Already Married in the Spirit: *Why You May Not be Married in the Natural*

by Dr. Marlene Miles
Freshwater Press 2024
freshwaterpress9@gmail.com

ISBN: 978-1-965772-41-6

Paperback Version

Table of Contents

Already Married in the Spirit:

Why You May Not Be Married in the Natural

Freshwater Press, USA

Introduction

The title of this book: **<u>Already Married in the Spirit</u>**: ***<u>Why You May Not Be Married in the Natural</u>*** could have alternately been subtitled, ***<u>Why You May Not Be Married in the Natural, or are Having a Hard Time in Your Marriage</u>***. However, that title would have been too long.

So please keep in mind that this book does not just apply to singles seeking to be married, but it is also spiritual help for marriages already in place. Even if you've reached your wit's end as to what is wrong with your relationship, God has the Wisdom to give you what you need when you've run out of "wit."

It is the Wisdom of God that is hopefully imparted to you through this book, since Wisdom is far superior to wit any day.

Making You Single

A few weeks ago, I heard the voice of the Lord and He said, **"I am making you single."**

What?

What does that even mean, Lord? I'm not currently married.

Silence.

Don't you love it when God sometimes shuts you up and makes you sit and be quiet, and think about what He just said, what you heard in your spirit? And, you know you heard it.

I recall a message many years ago where a pastor was teaching on being single. I don't remember all of her words, but her teaching was that we should be **whole** singles, not a half a person waiting for another person to make them whole. She stated that we need to be whole, sanctified singles so when the opportunity for marriage presents, we'll be ready. Well, there's nothing to disagree with there.

Saints of God, the rom com movie line, *"You complete me,"* is for the movies, not for real life. God created you, formed you, builds you up on your most holy faith, and He is the Author and Finisher of your faith. **God completes you**. So, if you are a grown person, don't remain incomplete waiting for someone to come along and complete you or make you over into something they want you to be; you are not a paper doll. Women, I am talking to you, but to men, also. And, men, do not think that you can turn a person into something that they are not to meet your specifications; women are not Play Doh or dolls that you can manipulate or play dress up with.

When it's time for marriage, take your complete self, connect with another complete person and you two marry and become **one.** That doesn't mean that either of you are perfect, but you are each a complete person, each of you with possession of your whole soul. That is if you want to form a proper, Godly covenant and to be successful in marriage.

Could that be what the Lord means?

Wow. I thought I was that already. Well, I must not be. Of course, God would know better than I would, else why would He be changing me, or asking me to change?

Unless--, He means something else. Unless He means that, **AND** something else. The Word of the Lord is often multipurpose, multifaceted, and multidimensional. Further, it transcends time. The Lord's saying to me, **I'm making you single**, could be true in many ways for many days, weeks, months, or even years.

There could be a myriad of meanings and possible outcomes to what the Lord meant when He said, **"I am making you single."**

Notable singles in the Bible were Mary, Martha, and Mary Magdalene. They were not made single; they were simply single.

Ruth was made single. Tamar was made single. Anna was single for many years, although she *had been* married, therefore she was also made single. Bathsheba was made single, by force. All the women who were made single went on to become impressive Bible figures. Ezekiel was made to be single.

Preparation

Esther got ready. It took her a year.

Before a young woman's turn came to go in to King Xerxes, she had to complete twelve months of beauty treatments prescribed for the women, six months with oil of myrrh and six with perfumes and cosmetics. (Esther 2:12 NIV)

Was the Lord endorsing spa and beauty treatments for me? I didn't know, but who could resist that kind of pampering and beautification? Esther's spa treatments were required by King Xerxes. The Bible doesn't say that this is what God instructed anyone to do. However, it was appointed unto Esther to please this king, so what was required by this earthly monarch was allowed by the Lord.

I know of various women who have had to hone certain skills to prepare to be a wife, and they followed the instruction of the Lord. But God didn't tell me to get ready to be married, He said, "I am making you single."

I also didn't get a timeline on this transformation from the Lord, so this will be ongoing until the Lord directs otherwise.

We should all look our best, but I have an aversion to the idea that a woman's only value is what she looks like. I resist the type of person who behaves as if he believes that. How does that person act?

Glad you asked; he's got a roving eye, he is idolatrous, his mouth is moving, and stupid things are coming out of it, fleshly things. He's never satisfied because the lust of the eye is never filled. This guy is shackled by the *spirit of whoredoms,* with idolatry, and celebrates it. The world celebrates flesh, so until the Word is preached to him, he will never think anything is wrong with this attitude.

A fellow once asked me what male actor I found especially attractive? I said, "No one," because I was married at the time, and I wasn't looking at any other male romantically. Plus, I don't fantasize about or idolize celebrities and TV personalities. The person who asked me was also married; I know this because he was married-- _to me,_ but that didn't seem to stop him from trying to fill his eyes, which we know can never be filled. Perhaps he thought I had that lustful eye problem too, but I did not. Thank God.

A man's only value is not in how he looks, either, except in the eyes of those who are carnal. Her looks could change tomorrow, or even later on today, and so could his. So, how is a carnal marriage supposed to last?

Have you ever noticed people who were obviously paired by their parents? That probably didn't take any preparation--, you just do as you're told, or be threatened to lose inheritance, or guilt-tripped into marrying the person that your parents want you to marry.

Those who have been matched by their parents may have been in their prime, in their twenties at the time and possibly gorgeous back then. By now, they are 50 or 60 years old, out after dinner taking a walk, but they are at least ½ a block away from one another. They appear to have no relationship; they have no conversation. They don't seem to have anything in common. I don't know if they don't like each other, or just don't know each other. They look so old and tired. When I see that I wonder how long their parents were happy to have obedient children who married strangers or someone they didn't even like just to please the parents. Doesn't it grieve the heart of a parent to see their child miserable, or unfulfilled and just going through the motions, while their life force is draining out of them?

These parents were obeying what some would call social norms to pair their child with someone who could provide for them financially. Their child's happiness? Was that ever a concern? Or was it all about duty as they indentured their child into a marriage that would produce children? *Marriage*? Hardly; it was more like slavery.

It's been years since this old couple was paired; they are no longer young, but are they pretty, handsome, and happy? Are they aging well? Folks, if you are happy, you will age well. You will age gracefully and beautifully. For Christians, marrying well is marrying the one that the Lord God has for you, and you two will become one, and the two of you can age together and still remain vibrant and lovely. Being in love makes you beautiful. Being connected to a person who doesn't care for you, such as a stranger, or someone you don't care for is draining; it's as though it consumes you.

When Abraham sent for a wife for Isaac, we believe he followed the mandates of God to choose that wife. The Bible does say that Isaac loved her, so there's that. However, there is nothing in the Bible that says the wife must love her husband. It says he should love his wife, but that the wife need only obey and submit to her husband.

Well, *what* husband?

Jesus is my husband; that's who I obey. Prophetically, Jesus should be husband to all of us and that's who we should obey.

Question: If you are a married woman and your husband is telling you, leading you, or causing you to sin, do you obey him when you know better? Or do you follow, believing you'll be fine, and God will punish the man only, while you go free because he led you into sin?

Complicated? I don't think so. Eve led Adam into sin, and both got cursed and kicked out of the Garden. Eve was wrong; Adam went along with the *wrong*. I will follow my husband if he is following Jesus. I will submit to the vision for the marriage. I will honor God when honoring any other human. Wouldn't anything else be sin?

The "*spouse*" the devil provides will do all the opposite of what a Godly spouse will bring to a marriage. We will get into more of this as this book progresses.

When parents don't love each other, it really affects their own lives as well as the lives of the kids. It's especially bad if the children know their doom is being planned by these parents who don't love each other. That doom is what they've seen their parents' relationship to be over the years, cold, loveless, or possibly worse. They too may have to marry someone their parents choose and suffer for the next 50 years-to-life.

God is better than that. Yes, God can matchmake, but He knows who He made you for, and who He made for you. Non-Christians who matchmake their children's marriages scare me. Therefore, I will seek to know and stick to the Lord's plan for my life, even if it means bucking tradition.

There are many plans in a man's heart,
Nevertheless the LORD's counsel—that will
stand. (Proverbs 19:21 NKJV)

Unmarried to Anyone or Anything

God said to me, **"I am making you single."** God's ways are not our ways, so is God saying that He will make me *un*married to anyone? And, I add, *anything?* This means that I will be solidly rid of all idols. Amen. Being rid of idols? I receive that. Amen.

When God sees me, He wants to see only me, not me with a bunch of idols like I'm a toddler who must always have a toy in my hand. Idols cannot enter into the presence of God, and I want and need to enter into His presence. Therefore, it would behoove all of us to drop the idols.

But if God is making me single that means that I am *un*single currently. That may also mean that I am married; but wouldn't I know if I were married? You would surely know if you were married---, wouldn't you?

Years ago, when in a horrible marriage, I had prayed and cried out to the Lord for a long time, lamenting that I wanted to break camp, but I did not want to break covenant.

Finally, one day the Lord answered my prayer, saying, **"I will divorce him for you."**

And so, He did. When God says a thing, it will come to pass.

Know ye not that the unrighteous shall not inherit the kingdom of God? Be not deceived: neither fornicators, nor idolaters, nor adulterers, nor effeminate, nor abusers of themselves with mankind,
Nor thieves, nor covetous, nor drunkards, nor revilers, nor extortioners, shall inherit the kingdom of God.
And such were some of you: but ye are washed, but ye are sanctified, but ye are justified in the name of the Lord Jesus, and by the Spirit of our God. (1 Corinthians 6:9-11)

Singly, I can enter into the presence of God. Singly, I can inherit the Kingdom of God. But encumbered with devils, demons, idols, and false *gods*, I cannot get in. None of us can.

How Can I Already Be Married?

How can I possibly be married and not know it? A couple can be married spiritually but not legally in a number of ways, including via:

- **The Commitment Ceremony**

This is a legally non-binding ceremony in which vows are made by a couple that they will spend their lives together. This is right up there with pinky swear, in my opinion.

- **The Spiritual Marriage**

A spiritual marriage that is performed in the natural by any type of priest or priestess from any type of religion. It could also be conducted by a real minister or pastor.

- **The Common Law Marriage**

Folks who shack up, have no marriage license, are basically living together. This is not a legal marriage. They usually also have not had a marriage ceremony of any kind.

- **The Evil Marriage**

An evil marriage can only be in place if evil covenants are also in place. In many cultures, when a child is born, they are wedded to the deities worshipped by their people. James Phred Kawalya has an amazing testimony of being wed to a 60-year-old witch at his birth, straight from the hospital. His mother was not allowed to take him home from the hospital until they first went to a certain village witch to marry the newborn off to the old lady. (https://www.youtube.com/watch?v=dvQvEtw2Izg&t=18s) Can you see how being married to a witch, a diviner, or a sorcerer made this newborn baby *that*, straight out of his mother's womb? When two become one, they become the same *one*. Whatever is strongest spiritually is what they become. If the baby has no spirituality, then the witch and witchcraft can easily overtake him.

What? know ye not that he which is joined to an harlot is one body? for two, saith he, shall be one flesh. (1 Corinthian 6:16)

It is not always a person that a baby or child is dedicated or married off to. Sometimes children are married to rivers, mountains, trees—all kinds of things. The parents may think they are buying protection for their child

18

because that is the way it's always been done in their culture, but it constitutes evil dedication and a spiritual marriage-- an evil spiritual marriage to be exact. After all, if a human is not marrying another human, that is not allowed by God; it is abomination.

When a person is married off to a deity, that is also an evil spiritual marriage. There are other forms of evil spiritual marriage, such as a *spirit* marrying a human with or without the human's consent and knowledge. Some of these spirit-to-human marriages are in effect at a person's birth, or soon thereafter. Such a case would be ancestral dedication.

A person could be their own reason for being married to an evil deity, by their own sin and iniquity where no other parent or relative is involved.

- Premarital sex invites a lot of demons into the party. With eyes to see what is happening <u>during</u> any sin, especially sexual sin, no one should want to participate in illegal sex, no matter how badly you *think* you want it.

Don't sin; get a hobby.

> Marriage is honorable among all, and the bed undefiled; but fornicators and adulterers God will judge. (Hebrews 13:4)

- Pornography/ Homosexuality are both illegal sex that invite untold numbers of demons.
- Ungodly places– if you go to a diviner, a psychic, a witch, a native doctor, etc., you are assigned a *familiar spirit,* that follows you home.
- Ungodly events such as festivals and demonic concerts are places where you may pick up a guardian demon, whether you want one or not. You are now their new home, and they believe they are now **married** to you.
- Demonic spiritual churches--, whether you know they are demonic or not, you will be assigned demons who believe they have **married** you.

Don't start none, won't be none is the best standard of practice, but if you've already stepped into sin and darkness, repent. Renounce the sin and the behavior. Denounce it. Ask the Lord for forgiveness and to remove the iniquity of the sin from you and your bloodline. Your goal is also to keep it from flowing into your generations. If you have married a demon, it's not just for you; it has married your family and bloodline. Do you want that demon hanging around for 3 or 4 or more generations in your family? A demon marriage is never just about you and the demon. It never is, unless you think demons are monogamous.

Of course, not. Get rid of it right away, and get the *ick* off of you that it may have brought to you by being in your life.

First, repent. After repentance, you may need to seek deliverance from a qualified, Godly deliverance minister. Then, walk upright before the Lord, perfecting holiness as much as it is possible. If there is no sin or iniquity in you, no curse can come upon you.

Like a darting sparrow, like a flying swallow, so an undeserved curse never arrives.
(Proverbs 26:2 CEB)

Puppy Love

Fantasy relationships where it is *just your imagination*, running away with you can invite a lot of problems into your life.

Everyone you fantasized about marrying, you may have married in the spirit. Everyone you sang about marrying because those were the words in the music of your day, you may have married. Those you thought about every time you heard or sung a certain song could have created a *spiritual spouse* for yourself. The *love you forevers* and all those covenant-making lyrics are a lot more impactful than you may have thought.

Could it be that you married someone when you first sang that song, or every time you sang that song? Could it be that you may have married another, or renewed the covenant when you sang it again?

Folks, secular song lyrics are for demonic purposes and CANNOT be devil proofed. Those songs are the perfect instrument to get you to state, recite, or sing the words that <u>make covenant</u> and marry a *spirit* being, such as a devil, demon, or an idol *god*. They are written and sung to become **traps** for all who sing them, not just the recording artist. Some of these songs are called trap songs and for good reason, not the reason you think.

This is one of the reasons we should not love the world. There is no real Love in the things of the world.

Love not the world, neither the things *that are* in the world. If any man love the world, the love of the Father is not in him. (1 John 2:15)

Not too long ago I caught myself singing a song that had been my favorite for years. Are you kidding? It was in my key— whatever key that is, and I could hit the notes. It was a love song, and it was about----, that's when I caught myself, it was about soul ties, and love lost, and sudden attractions, and fornication, basically. I stopped singing immediately and began to listen. Those lyrics were marine kingdom lyrics all the way. Then I looked into the song library of that artist and realized that all her songs were marine kingdom songs that were not able to be devil proofed, because the devil either wrote them or told the person who wrote them what to write.

She's not the only singer working for the marine kingdom, after all they run the music industry. Isn't it a common complaint of secular artists that they can't use their own songs and that they are **told** what to sing?

Now you know.

With your sanctified self, you cannot bless a secular song written by, and for marine kingdom purposes. You cannot bless what God has cursed, and vice versa.

Wasn't the devil in charge of worship and music in Heaven before he got kicked out? The Bible says that the devil took 1/3 of the stars (fallen angels) when he fell. I'll venture to say that he also took the music, or as much of it as he could take with him.

So, every love song you keep singing over and again to somebody or *nobody* is really to the idol that wrote it, inspired it. You then fall into agreement with the 30 witches who work for the music industry who pray over certain songs so the people will like, buy, and download that music to make them into hits.

You cannot bless what God has cursed.

Saints of God can we get 30 people together and in agreement, on a regular basis in a prayer meeting? Shouldn't it be more desired to come together for good than for evil? By singing the lyrics to these songs you may have already gotten married, quite a number of times, actually, in the spirit. I pray that God will make you **single**, also in the sense of your not being married in the spirit to any demons, devils, fallen angels, idol *gods*, or Satan.

In the spirit, you may be married to everyone you *almost* married, but perhaps you got cold feet, or they jilted you, but if evil soul ties were created, you are still connected to them. An evil soul tie is as if you're married to them. You may not be married in the natural, but in the spirit, you are. And that could be exactly why you are not married in the natural.

Every soul tie that is tied to you potentially married you. Soul ties can start out as emotional and lead to other levels of being soul tied. In the natural, maybe no one can *see* a soul tie, but they may sense that you have *emotional baggage* from previous relationships. Yeah, that preoccupation with your ex is picked up by people, whether they know what to call it or not.

Emotional Marriages

Emotional marriages, whether in the past or present, as in soul ties, to people that you are not and should not be married to are evil. Emotional cheating is a thing, and it is not good.

Work spouse relationships, for example, are close, platonic bonds with co-workers whom you feel you have a lot in common with. Folks, if you need your spouse or a spouse all day long--, if you need a babysitter all day, if you can tolerate your own spouse all day long, then get a job together or start a business together and be close, love each other to pieces. Keep strangers out of that area of your soul. I say that because you wouldn't want your own spouse to have a work spouse--, or would you?

How about a church spouse?

What?

Your own spouse doesn't go to church or doesn't go to the one you go to, but he has "friends" at that church, and they are very close. How does that make you feel?

Be satisfied with your own spouse and leave others out of the marriage portion of your life. If you can have an emotional support animal with you, then there should be no problem bringing your own spouse to work, church, or wherever you go.

Of course, if you are using your work spouse to do your work for you, that's another whole thing. There are a lot of people who can't do their own job, so they buddy up with a competent person and manipulate that buddy-spouse, work-spouse or whatever you call them to do their job for them.

For example, a young woman came to work for me at my office. She was determined that her friend needed a new job as well. Eventually I interviewed and hired the second girl because I could see she was much smarter and more competent than the first. Within two weeks, the smarter one was no longer doing her assigned job, she was doing the job of the friend who had told her about the opening at my office in the first place. I then found out that the first one couldn't do most of what was on her resume that got her hired.

Later, I realized the first lady was obsessed with the smarter one. They must enter the building together, they must have lunch together, they must leave the building together at the end of the day. All this was on the insistence of the first employee. Still, it was weird. So weird that after they left my employ the smarter girl moved out of state. Then we found out that the first girl, her husband and five kids also moved to the same city the smart girl moved to.

But the first girl really couldn't do the job, and that was discovered when the lines were drawn as to job description. The smarter girl fared well, and the first girl floundered.

I've seen more than one case of the person who can't use the computer or navigate the software, in their respective workplaces, so they buddy up to someone, usually of the opposite gender, using powers of seduction as they try to *nice* their way into getting what they want from the more competent person. One is using the other, but the other thinks a relationship is budding. These are *seducing* and *lying spirits*, but the one who "likes" the other may become emotionally attached, or even *spiritually married* to their work crush. The seducer doesn't care spiritually, he is just making it through another day in a job that he is not qualified to do.

Work spouse? Why can't it just be, *co-worker*? The designation of spouse should be given to your spouse, only. The treatment you would give a spouse should only be given to your spouse. Period.

Everyone should be an adult at your workplace, but the lines are sure to get blurred. We're talking about humans here; the lines will get blurred, and signals may get crossed. The man, for example, who believes the young lady to be his *work spouse* is one thing, but what does the lady think?

She may be thinking, *I do everything for him. He needs me. He should leave his wife, and we can be together.* It happens too often. I think of the woman who had a framed picture of the pastor of our church on her desk at work. She had claimed the pastor as her husband; well, at least everyone at that office thought that's who he was to her. When the truth came out, everyone was shocked.

Everyone you dated and had sex with you married, since *goes into* equals married, spiritually. **You are still married to them if you haven't <u>spiritually</u> divorced them.**

Everyone you didn't date, but had sex with you are married to, unless you have **<u>spiritually</u>** divorced them.

Everyone you thought the two of you were dating, when you had sex with them, you married them, spiritually. Some can have a genuine fondness for another and never should cross the line of fondness into sex, but once you do, even once--, you've married them.

Everyone you married – whether you are married now or not, if you haven't divorced them **<u>spiritually</u>**, then you are still married to them. This and all of the above could be why you are not married or attracting marriage partners today.

A beautiful woman goes to the track every day to jog a few miles with her friend--, a married man. They have not crossed any sexual lines, but she is seen as a married woman because she is always with that man at the track. It is just the two of them; his wife does not join in the exercise program. The single jogging lady is in shape and beautiful, but she wonders why she hasn't met any potential men who would be suitable or interested in her for marriage.

You don't have to date everyone that you are fond of, or become obsessed with or have sex with them, or become obsessed with everyone that you date, or wish to marry them. You can just be friends or close friends.

Everyone who married *you* and you know nothing about it--, you are potentially married in the spiritual realm and thereby being blocked in the natural realm from a natural marriage.

Why this is so weird is that the devil doesn't follow any Christian rules unless he can twist them to his advantage. Do you think the devil cares if someone commits adultery? Why, no; he would encourage sexual sin of any kind. Then why should he care to enforce a "spiritual marriage" that will block a natural marriage, as if you're cheating on a *spirit spouse*? Yeah, that's the answer, it is to block a natural marriage.

For this reason, we must know that a natural marriage is of God, desired by God, mandated by God, and has Godly purpose in it. As well, not getting married in the natural, and staying married steals from that couple because **God has wedding and marriage gifts for them.**

Dream marriages are not always the foretelling of your real marriage. Sometimes dream marriages are very dangerous because you may not know **who** you just married. *Spirit spouse* and other devils are famous for the dream masquerade, they must be, after all *spirit spouse* may be 2000 years old for all you know. Pray against demonic dreams every day if you have to. Some demonic dreams don't seem demonic; don't be deceived. Pray against demonic dreams daily.

1. Every demonic dream, whether I remember them or not, I bring them all under the Blood of Jesus. I declare that they will fall to the ground as dead works and come to nothing, in the Name of Jesus. Amen.

Pimped Out in the Spirit

Every vow or oath of love and *I will love you forever* you spoke may have married you to the person you spoke it to, or about. They may not have even been present in the same space as you, if you were fantasizing like a lovestruck high school teen. You may have married them whether you realize it or not. Whether they even know you or not, you got married. I'll clarify by saying you may not have married them; you married the *representation* of who you think you married. Fantasy *spirit spouse* is real, even though it's a fantasy. You married a demon, but you think you bonded or drew closer to that person that you love or are hot for.

Then one day you forgot you married that person; but you are still married to the demon that came in because of your fantasy--, unless you have **spiritually** divorced that demon. Unlikely, since you don't even know that you married anything or anyone, and certainly not a demon.

Well you don't know yet--. In subsequent chapters we will list how to know.

Later, you may have met another heartthrob, and you did the same thing all over again. Do you realize how many times you may have repeated this, even without *rinsing* first? Do you know how many times you have repeated this, working yourself up into a *lather* without even rinsing?

Do you yet see how many *husbands* or *wives* you may have? Unless you've done your spiritual housekeeping and divorced them all--, each and every one of them.

Soul-tie-making vows have bound you to whomever was the object of your desire at that time. Have you broken any evil soul ties? Then they still exist. The soul ties with living people are especially long-standing if gifts were involved, coming from either direction.

People who have claims on you that you know nothing about—just as you did it to your secret crush, others may have done it to you.

Entities may have claims on you because of your own unrepentant sin that allowed demons, devils, and idols into your life. Those spiritual entities may have come in through your ancestors and are in your foundation or bloodline. Or, if you are in sin, especially sexual sin, or saddled with iniquity from any source, and you've angered a witch, warlock, or any evil human agent, you could have been married off to Lord knows who or Lord knows what, and still not know that you are married in the spirit. These are more reasons as to why you may not be available or seen as <u>available</u> to be married in the natural realm.

Worse, are you being pimped out in the spirit, in your dream life? If you are having sex in the dream, how many different faces are there? That's how many different *spouses* you may have—defiling you every night, or on some other schedule.

To become **single**, you will need to divorce each of them. **If that's what the Lord means by making me single, I'm all for that.** A *spirit spouse* is dangerous, and some are called hidden *spirit spouses* – they don't want to have sex with you, but you also don't know that they are there, unless the Spirit of God *tells* you so.

Only God can make you *single* of all of that.

The Lord allows divorce.

2. Lord, in the Name of Jesus show me if I have a *spirit spouse*, and how many there are.
3. Lord, in the Name of Jesus show me if I have *spirit children* and how many there are.
4. Lord, show me how to get rid of them and be fully delivered so that I can be completely **single** again to serve You and be in a Godly natural, successful, happy marriage, in Jesus' Name.

If you're married in the spirit this is an **arranged marriage**—arranged by Satan. In a spirit marriage you are not special; you are a commodity, a thing, something to be used. Trash. *Spirit spouse* doesn't love you; he or she is incapable of it, and is never suitable as a husband or wife. *Spirit spouse* will lead you into constant defilement and straight to hell. Don't put up with this. The devil doesn't love you and can never be your husband. He will lead you into sin and you will incur curses because of it. This is just like the person who wants to "date" you, but never marry you in the natural. That person will only lead you into sin, you will incur curses, losses, and eventually death and hell.

The wrong "spouse" in the natural or in the spirit doesn't have anything in common with you. What communion does Light have with Darkness? They won't take time to get to know you or be a physical, financial or emotional support to you. No, quite the opposite; they are an emotional, spiritual, and financial drain. You will not age well with the wrong spouse; you may look old before time. As a matter of fact, *spirit spouse* can MAKE you look older than you are to keep you from being attractive to potential suitors in the natural. It will grieve you, as the victim, and it will grieve others who really love you to see you miserable. But the wrong spouse does not care one iota.

Marriage? Hardly, it is more like slavery.

Married to Idols

In the same way can you see how many *idols* you could be married to? You may have believed in luck as a kid. You may have played with an 8-Ball or a Ouija Board as a kid. You may have looked up your horoscope every day or every month for years since the disclaimer at the bottom of that article or video said this was, *For entertainment only*. Entertainment? Can't be any harm in that, right?

Wrong.

You may have gone to a mystic at the beach one summer on vacation, just for fun. You believed in New Age as a teenager and collected crystals. You may have grown up with a relative who believed in all kinds of superstitions such as salt over the shoulder, black cats, ladders ---, all kinds of old wives' tales and beliefs. Do you have any idea how many *idols* are connected to all of that?

You believe in this, that, or the other –
changing churches or even changing religions
often. How many *idols* have you collected in
your life? Have you **divorced** all of them?
Have you divorced *any* of them?

Territorial demons, demons in general
want to marry everyone--, all the women in a
"territory." Genesis 6 reads, *And they took as
many to wife as they desired,* therefore, these
entities will marry you if you are from their
region of authority. It is dangerous to invoke
the name of idols and devils, and demons. If
you call on them, use them, ask them for
anything--, anything at all, you owe them. In
jest, a person could say the "football *gods*" or
the "cooking *gods*"—you are actually praying
to and invoking them. Stop playing.

When you ask for things that God
doesn't give, such as ungodly things, you are
praying to an *idol* whether you know it or not.
Thanking your lucky stars? There's a *god* for
that. When you give them attention, praise or
worship in any way they believe that you owe
them and will attempt to marry you.

And in all *things* that I have said unto you be
circumspect: and make no mention of the
name of other gods, neither let it be heard
out of thy mouth. (Exodus 23:13)

Every Time You Had Sex You Got Married

It's that old, W*hich came first, the chicken or the egg?,* thing again. Did you get married and then consummate the marriage? Or, did you, by consummation get yourself married? *Goes into* equals married in the spirit, so any raggedy old demon that had sex with you, even in the spirit, has **married** you.

5. Wedding day fantasy, childhood crushes and *pretend* marriages be cancelled now, in the Name of Jesus.
6. I divorce every person or actor that ever stood up with me or beside me in any play, movie, skit, or enactment--, even at church, in Jesus' Name.
7. Lord, restore me to the perfect way you created me to be. Restore my soul, in the Name of Jesus.

8. Lord, restore my body, health, and strength, in the Name of Jesus.

9. Lord, restore my spirit; renew in me a right spirit, in the Name of Jesus.

10. Lord, make me single and whole. If I am single and ready to be in a Kingdom marriage, thank You, Lord.

11. Lord, if I'm already married in the natural, make me, and make our marriage a Kingdom marriage, in Jesus' Name.

12. Lord, expose all enemies in the natural and spiritual realms against me and my marriage.

13. Holy Spirit give me that now. Give me what and how to pray about it, in Jesus' Name.

14. Lord, please forgive me. I forgive my parents and ancestors for evil dedication whether they were tricked, duped, ignorant or greedy.

15. Please Lord, release me from every evil dedication, in the Name of Jesus.

16. Lord, forgive me for all personal sin that is given ground to the enemy, especially sexual sin, in the Name of Jesus.

17. I break all satanic connections and linkage to strange people in the dream, in the Name of Jesus.
18. I remove the right that the enemy took from me to keep me from getting married, by the power in the Blood of Jesus. (X3)
19. Lord, I take back all my sexual rights that the enemy has usurped, in the Name of Jesus.
20. Angels of the Only Living God, remove every blockage to my Kingdom marriage, in the Name of Jesus.
21. All masquerading *spirits* troubling my dreams and marital life, be bound, in the Name of Jesus.
22. I receive my Kingdom match, in the Name of Jesus.
23. Thank You, Lord.
24. Lord, turn away all that will jilt, disappoint, or fail me, in the Name of Jesus.
25. Do not let me marry the assignment of the devil, Lord.
26. Do not let me marry the assignment of the devil, Lord.
27. Do not let me marry the assignment of the devil, in Jesus' Name.

28. Lord, send me a spouse that will be hot in prayers, individually and at the family altar, in Jesus' Name.
29. Lord, make me mindful that the foundation I was born into greatly affects my life, the life of my spouse and ultimately the life of our child. Deliver us, O Lord, in Jesus' Name.
30. I cover myself with the Blood of Jesus
31. Lord, release me from inherited iniquity and bondage, in the Name of Jesus.
32. Lord, thank You that I can be delivered from any violation, that nothing is too hard for You, in the Name of Jesus.
33. Lord, I confess my sins and the sins of my ancestors, especially those linked to evil powers. Lord, forgive, in the Name of Jesus.
34. Lord, I break the sequela of polygamy off my family and household, in the Name of Jesus.
35. Lord, blot out the iniquity from all the sins of my forefathers, by the precious Blood of Jesus.
36. Lord, hear my repentance. Remove the curse--, all the curses, in the Name of Jesus.
37. Lord, let Your Word perform in my life.

38. Lord, avenge me my adversaries, in the Name of Jesus.

39. The God of Elijah who answers by Fire, answer me by Fire, in the Name of Jesus.

40. God who calls those things that be not as though they were, answer me by Fire, in the Name of Jesus.

41. Lord, blot out every satanic deposit in my life, in my body, in the mighty Name of Jesus Christ.

42. Lord, anything that makes Your promise fail in my life, let it be destroyed with Fire. Amen.

43. Evil vows that I've spoken in jest or that others have led me to speak thinking it's funny, I renounce them all, in Jesus' Name

44. I renounce them all whether spoken knowingly or while I wasn't even aware of it, in the Name of Jesus.

45. Lord, deliver me from all word curses that I've spoken out of my own mouth, especially those pertaining to marriage, in the Name of Jesus.

46. *To die for?* **Nothing is to die for.** Lord, forgive me; I renounce and denounce ever speaking those evil words at any time, in Jesus' Name.

47. Forgive me Lord for all the times I've said anti-life or fruitless words over my own body, life, marriage, children, job or business, in the Name of Jesus.

48. Lord, I break every covenant with any sex demon, especially from the evil water Kingdom.

49. Water *spirits* that trouble my dream life, die, in the Name of Jesus.

50. I bind and paralyze every astral projecting power from entering my home, my bed, or me, in the Name of Jesus.

51. I bind and reject the *spirit of the dog* from my soul, spirit, and body, in the Name of Jesus.

52. Lord, set Your ministering angels all around me, in the Name of Jesus.

53. I renounce, break, and *loose* my body, which is the temple of the Holy Spirit from the grip of the kingdom of darkness. Be redeemed, cleansed, sanctified, and set aside, in Jesus' Name.

54. All *spirits* attached to my bondage, come out of me, come out of my womb, come out of my reproductive organs with all your roots, in Jesus' Name.

55. Get out *spirit spouse*, in the Name of Jesus. (X3 or more)

56. Every marriage in the spiritual realm blocking or interfering with my real marriage in the physical, be destroyed by the Flaming Sword of the Lord.

57. Every marriage-scattering devil, demon or idol, die, in the Name of Jesus.

58. Get lost, *spirit children*. I don't want you; you're not welcome in my life. Get out, in the Name of Jesus.

59. *Spirit spouse* of any origin, I terminate your access to my dream and physical life. No more access to me, by FIRE, in the Name of Jesus.

60. The power that does not belong in my bed, but is in love with my bed, let my bed become Fire to you, in the Name of Jesus.(X3)

61. My whole bed is the Blood of Jesus. My whole bed is the Blood of Jesus. My whole bed is the Blood of Jesus.

62. Lord, whatever I've been doing that gives invitation or power to *spirit spouse*, I stop it now. I stop it now, I stop it now, in the Name of Jesus.

63. I denounce it. I renounce it, in Jesus' Name. Lord, forgive me, Amen.

64. Anti-faithfulness powers, die, from my father's house, die with your *whoredoms*, in the Name of Jesus.

65. Lord, I pray against unfriendly friends, evil relatives, stealth enemies up against me, my marriage, my spouse, my child, in Jesus' Name.

66. I pray against the demonic initiation by the evil laying on of hands, in the Name of Jesus.

67. Tainted natural or spiritual food, be vomited and have no negative effect on me, by the Blood of Jesus.

68. I curse every fibroid to die, spiritually, by Fire, by Fire, by Fire, in the Name of Jesus. (X5 or more). Never return, in the Name of Jesus.

69. God, send correction now, in the Name of Jesus.

70. Infections brought on by *spirit spouse*, polyps, et cetera, be healed now, in the Name of Jesus.

71. Every hidden illness in my body, be healed. My body be made whole now, in the Name of Jesus.

72. Wet dream, any sex in the dream, I terminate you by the power of God in Jesus Christ.

73. Issues in my reproductive system as a result of spirit marriage, Lord Jesus, heal them, flush them out, in Jesus' Name.

74. Witchcraft powers attacking me in any way, Hailstones of Fire, bombard those powers, defeat to death, in the Name of Jesus,

75. I take back my eggs from every evil hand, in the Name of Jesus, I take back my eggs from every evil hand, in the Name of Jesus. I take back my eggs from every evil hand, in the Name of Jesus.

76. I recover all lost sperm from every evil seed thief, in the Name of Jesus. (X3)

77. Lord, I repent for all spilled seed, in the Name of Jesus.

78. Father, reverse all defilement that has been perpetrated against me, in the Name of Jesus.

79. Lord, I boldly send all live spiritual ammo sent against me back to sender, in Jesus' Name.

80. I break every curse placed on me because of jealousy by jealous exes, jealous friends, current and former coworkers, associates,

jealous family members, jealous strangers and enemies, in Jesus' Name.

81. I break every medical curse against me, in Jesus' Name.

82. I break every curse issued by satanic ministers, in the Name of Jesus.

83. I break every curse emanating from evil prophecies, in the Name of Jesus.

84. I break every evil initiation over my life, in the Name of Jesus.

85. I break every evil dedication over my life, in the Name of Jesus.

86. I break every evil spiritual marriage that has ever included me, in the Name of Jesus.

87. I bind every retaliatory *spirit* and command all backlash against me because of these prayers to backfire to infinity, in Jesus' Name.

88. I seal all these declarations across every age, realm, and dimension and timeline past, present, and future, in the mighty Name of Jesus Christ. Amen, Amen, and **Amen.**

Married Off in the Spirit

Evil dedication.

Do you remember the child's story of Rumpelstiltskin? A girl had to spin straw into gold, but she needed help and got it from an entity named Rumpelstiltskin. To even the score, the elfin creature told the girl that if she couldn't guess his name, he would get her first born. *Really*? Those fairy tales are not fairy tales, people. If the man's name wasn't guessed correctly that firstborn child would have been dedicated or promised to Rumpelstiltskin.

Freemasons do a symbolic wedding; they think it's cute...it's not. It is demonic because Freemasonry is demonic. They will marry little boys or girls in what looks like a bring your kid to work day. It's really some kind of ceremony done at a certain level of freemasonry. It's not adorable. Freemasonry is satanic, so if your child was involved in this, *who* do you think your child married? If it was you, *who* do you think you married?

Tom Thumb weddings were done as fund raisers--, at least they were back in the day. The danger here is obvious, but also know that around nine years old is a very perilous age, especially for little girls; it's a choice age for occultic initiation and indoctrination. Parents and those who want to be parents keep your eyes on your kids all the time. Don't let them go just anywhere and stay with just anyone. Seek guidance and the Wisdom of the Lord regarding away trips and sleepovers, especially.

Yeah, the kids may be innocent, but the demons that may influence them or others are not.

So where are the blessings of being married going if you are not married in the natural? Stolen? How are they stolen?

Ishmael, the son of Abraham received the blessings of Abraham **without** being the child of covenant. *Spirit spouses* can make *spirit children* who partake of **your** blessings because they are **your** offspring – and you don't even know they exist. (Talk about child support). So, if unholy alliances are made with demons, devils, succubus, incubus, and et cetera, they can partake of or completely steal your blessings, completely against your knowledge and against your will. But if you are willfully doing this, that is, spreading your Grace, giving that which is holy to the unholy, this is abomination.

WHY do these demons want to marry you?

Like a boxer or a wrestler tying up his opponent, being married to a demon in the spirit is to keep you from exerting your own power and authority, singly and as a united married couple. It's to limit you. To block you. It's not just because you're pretty or handsome or both, it is to steal from you. It is to steal, kill and destroy. There is no respect of persons or age; demons will come at anyone at any time, as soon as they can. If you have a certain Grace on you and a promising future in the Lord, they will be after you. They will come after your crown, your glory, your star, all designed to tie you up so you don't fulfill destiny.

For we wrestle not against flesh and blood, but against principalities, against powers, against the rulers of the darkness of this world, against spiritual wickedness in high places. (Ephesians 6:12)

I am not an expert on wrestling, but the verse above tells us that **wrestling is happening in the spirit**. Two things I know that if you are tied up by a wrestler, you are stagnated or delayed from progress. And, I also know that if you are pinned down in wrestling, the opponent can have his way against you. Sleep paralysis is a pinning down, and it is a common *spirit spouse* move. This verse further tells me that we shouldn't worry so much about what human beings are doing as we do about what is happening in the spirit and in the dream.

It is what happens in the dream that has the impact in the natural far more than what is happening in the natural world affecting the spirit world. If you get your spirit life right, then the natural world must follow, and also be right. Amen.

God doesn't waste, He doesn't pour out on the ground, but if something is coming to you from God, it must come from Third Heaven and traverse second heaven and that's where the seat of Satan and his throne is. This is how and where things get intercepted--, in the spirit realm. In your *wrestling*, if you are tied up or pinned down, how will you receive from the Lord? Defiling you sexually blocks your blessings from ever reaching you. Worse, the demon that tied you up, that defiled you, blocked your blessing then got your blessing, while you got nothing, ***but defiled***.

In defiling you, having sex with you, marrying you, you became **one** with that foul *spirit*. Do you realize that you became every foul thing that *spirit* is? By that attack, sin was forced upon you. You are not Jesus who became sin for us, and there is no redemption for devils and demons, so, there was no reason for you to have taken on the sin of the sex demon.

Folks, this happens in the natural with demon-laden people as well. It is not just the spiritual marriages that you should be concerned about.

After defilement, more than ever, and immediately, you need Jesus to bear these foul flesh works and sins away from you. you need Jesus to cleanse and wash you, forgive you and blot out all this iniquity.

This is no different than a rapist impregnating his victim; he gave the victim something, or some things that she never ever wanted, at least not his brand of those things.

Are you ready to pray and repent, yet?

Turned Over

If you are under an evil dedication, it means your life and destiny have been turned over to the devil, with or without your knowledge. It could have been at birth, after you were born, when you were a young child, and you knew nothing about it. It could have been *before* you were born. It could have been *before* you were conceived; it could have been a *condition* of a conception ritual that one or both parents did to even get pregnant with you. That condition would be that the child now *belongs* to the idol (devil, demon) that helped them conceive.

It would be great to believe that you are righteous seed, but we don't know what folks have done to get the things they desired or felt that they needed--, even our own relatives.

If you have been "dedicated" that means that Satan has full control over your life.

Your parents could have innocently, ignorantly, or by tradition, tried to protect you by dedicating you to some *idol* that is known in their world to protect children and babies. People get dedicated to family or community idols. Those idols may include serpents, marine deities, idol *gods, or other evil spirits* that pose as good and helpful. Unless a person is a satanist or occultist, and at a certain level in a cult, the true identity of the *"gods'* they deal with is usually hidden.

89. Lord, release my life from every evil dedication by the power in the Blood of Jesus.
90. I release my life from every evil dedication, by the power in the Blood of Jesus.

Some types of evil dedication include the following:
- Water dedication
- Coven dedication
- Tree dedication
- Blood dedication
- Marriage dedication
- Sexual dedication
- Demonic dream dedication
- Evil marks dedication

- Curse dedication

How can you know if you've been dedicated?

Pray, ask the Lord and listen. The Holy Spirit will tell and or show you either in your waking life, or in a dream. Suspect evil dedication if any of these things are happening to you:

- Your life is crazy and seems out of control.
- Your dream life seems afflicted. For instance, you may be summoned all over the place in your sleeping life.
- Your marital destiny is affected or afflicted.
- Nothing is working out where you live; territorial powers are ruling you.

You could be part of a collective captivity, as dedications affect families, towns, neighborhoods, cities, even nations, and whole continents.

- You feel controlled or manipulated in life.

91. Every evil power controlling my life, release me and die, in the Name of Jesus.
92. Lord, release my life from every evil dedication, by the power in the Blood of Jesus.
93. I release my life from every evil dedication by the power in the Blood of Jesus.

Another sign of evil dedication is you are drawn to evil – well, you don't see evil as evil, you see demonic symbols, images, even satanic jewelry as something desirable to have. Somehow these things and images attract you, and you don't resist acquiring them. If you objectively look around your house and life you may find demonic symbols everywhere--, if you have been dedicated. And you don't see a thing in the world wrong with it.

I've seen a parade of spider tattoos, dragons, snakes, and other witchy and occultic things on a daily basis. No one forced these tattoos on the people; it's not like they were branded as slaves or property. But they desired to "brand" themselves, and they chose demonic images to place permanently on their own skin.

Ignorantly, a person could choose a totally satanic tattoo that they think is cool, and by having it on their skin, they draw a demon to him or herself. When you tattoo yourself, you mark yourself and when demons see the mark, you are identified as one of *theirs*. So then they come for you. They stay because they think they have married you. If you are already married in the spiritual realm, then how will you find or be able to marry your real spouse? Married in the spirit blocks you from getting married in the natural world. *Spirit spouse* and those other demons will fight you. They can put you in evil timelines so you miss divine connections, but if you happen to meet the right person that you are supposed to marry, the demons will fight you and they will fight the person who is interested in you, as well.

Jabez was given an evil name. But there are way worse names than Jabez. Find out what your name really means; change it if you have to. Your name may be a reflection of your having been dedicated, or your dedication chose your name. Your name, if it is an evil name, can also draw evil *spirits*. What names are you calling in your house? Does your child, or even your pet have an evil name? Find out and change it because **every time you call that**

name you are summoning the demon associated with that name.

Some of the things that we don't even think twice about can initiate or dedicate a person. Throwing money in a wishing well is throwing offerings to the evil marine kingdom. Now they think you came to play–, after all, you gave a sacrifice. Throwing food, garments or other things into rivers or bodies of water is also sacrificing to idols, especially if you are making a wish or requesting something from the deity, even something as vague as *luck*.

- Ritualistic bathing in rivers, the ocean, and other waters.
- Sitting under a marine kingdom pastor or priest knowingly or unknowingly.

Certain festivals, such as marine festivals, or serpent dedication festivals can initiate or dedicate a person of any age. Some you don't even have to guess about, such as the Festival of the Steel Phallus in Japan; people take their children to these festivals. And there are other festivals that initiate and renew evil dedication.

Sleeping on white cloth given to you by fetish priests, sorcerers, witch doctors, and demonic "pastors." The wearing of certain garments, especially being a part of a white garment church. Any ritual can initiate a person.

Halloween. You don't have to dress as the bride of Frankenstein or the bride of anything, but just by being out on Halloween in any get up and participating in the festival initiates you or renews evil covenants with the dark kingdom. Satan will gladly send you and evil *spirit spouse*, or marry you himself.

The carved Jack-O-Lantern on your doorstep tells Satan that he can have your youngest. To the devil "having" implies **marriage**. Are you the youngest in your family? Did you all carve pumpkins for Halloween? This is nothing to play with; you've got some praying to do.

Don't stop praying, saying, and declaring:

94. I release my life from every evil initiation by the power in the Blood of Jesus.
95. I release my life from every evil dedication by the power in the Blood of Jesus.

96. I am married to Jesus, Satan leave me alone, in the Name of Jesus.
97. I bear in my body the marks of the Lord Jesus Christ, by the power in the Blood of Jesus, I declare Jesus is my husband, and I am not or any longer married to any devil, demon, idol, false *god*, or Satan, in the Name of Jesus.
98. I snatch my child back from the clutches of the devil because of evil initiations that I was not aware of, or dedications made in ignorance or accidentally, in the Name of Jesus. I declare my child will serve the only Living God, and never Satan, in the Name of Jesus.

Do Not Let This Happen

Don't let things just happen to you without being aware that these things are ungodly and indicate that you should take action.

- Anti-progress, especially spiritually where you haven't been able to be saved, or hear God, receive the Holy Spirit, or enter into worship.
- Anti-destiny events where everything you do seems to be blocked, delayed, or stagnant, especially your spiritual purpose.
- .Reproach where you should be appreciated or even celebrated.
- Closed heavens; toiling with little to no results.
  Life is hard, instead of life is good, or **Life is God**.

- One step forward, two steps back; rising and falling.
- Untimely, and or violent and sudden death.
- Chronic sicknesses.
- *Almost there* syndrome all the time – if it weren't for bad luck syndrome.
- Evil timelines, missed opportunities, missed connections, and missed blessings.
- *Anti-marriage* where you can't seem to meet or successfully date or get engaged to anyone.
- *Anti-marriage–*, you are married but things aren't going well.

Saints of God, if you are already married to any power that you were dedicated to, any and all of these things could be happening to you. Don't do nothing. Don't just lament. Fight!

- The *spirit of error* and mistakes rules you and can ruin you.
- Financial and reproductive barrenness.

The *spirit of the dog* can come upon you causing extreme *lust* and leading to sexual idolatry, depending on what idol you were dedicated to. Marine demons tend to be sexual in nature.

If you're spiritually married now, in an evil marriage, then these things may also be happening to you *spiritually*. Covering cast. Evil veil. No one can see you. These demons can make you look ugly, old, or unappealing to your real Kingdom spouse, whom you may actually know and be friends with. They put you in an evil timeline and you may miss divine connections of many kinds. Yes, meeting the right person. Getting an education, so you will be ready when you meet the right person. They interfere with your career so you may meet the right person and know it, but you may be broke, so you two may not get married in the natural.

Even if you get married, these evil demons don't stop there. Remember, if you've been dedicated to them, they believe they are married to you; they are very jealous and very territorial. Think of the worst abusive spouse that you've ever heard of – they are worse than that. These demons will keep oppressing and harassing you, calling on other demons to help them if necessary. They believe they are married to you and have every right to be there, until you **DIVORCE** them and **make** them go away. If not, they will go on and on until they can break you up. If they can't destroy your marriage, they will attempt to make you or you two miserable in that marriage.

Countless blessings are stolen from those who do not marry. Those who are not fruitful and multiplying in marriage are being robbed.

Marriage *is to be held* in honor among all [that is, regarded as something of great value], and the *marriage* bed undefiled [by immorality or by any sexual sin]; for God will judge the sexually immoral and adulterous. (Hebrews 13:4)

Whoso findeth a **wife** findeth a good thing, and obtaineth favour of the Lord. (Proverbs 18:22)

95. I am a success and not a failure, in the Name of Jesus.

96. Every power of rising and falling in my life, break and die by the power in the Blood of Jesus.

97. Lord, release my life from every evil dedication by the power in the Blood of Jesus.

Spirit Guide

Then there are those who are totally deceived. Some believe they have a *spirit guide*. I recently saw online where someone decided they were in love with their *spirit guide* and wanted to marry it. There is no angel that will marry you, except a fallen angel, and that is a demon. A *spirit guide* is a demon. It is a *familiar spirit*. It could be a monitoring *spirit*. By any name, it already believes it is married to you.

If you are now married in the spirit, these demons are territorial, devilish, mean and they will block you from having a natural spouse. Further, what spouse would put up with you and your make-believe friend that they cannot see?

A man retells the story of sleeping over at a friend's house after a night at the bar but in the next room he could hear his friend saying things like, Stop it! No! ... The owner of that house where they slept over had a *spirit spouse* that was attacking him in the night.

Depending on what you practice as a "religion," you may be already married to a *spirit*, a person, or even an animal. Shamans and many other "religions" believe in getting married in the spirit. They adopt a spirit animal, and they believe in *spirit spouses*, as do some other religions in the world.

Priests who say they are married to Jesus and therefore do not marry in the natural seem to understand spirit marriage precludes marriage in the natural which is the point of this book. And it is something the devil is incessantly trying to enforce against humankind.

This does not mean that a married person cannot have or get a *spirit spouse*. What it means is there is going to be a fight if this happens. Who wins is determined by your discernment to know what is happening spiritually and not just blame problems on your natural spouse then fight it out to a natural divorce. It depends on your relationship with the Lord, and your determination to win and get **single** by getting rid of *spirits* that believe they have married you.

It would be so sad to get divorced in the natural because of *spirit spouse* and still have *spirit spouse*, rather than getting rid of *spirit spouse* and keeping your natural marriage.

Ancestors

The dead know nothing. Whatever spirit or *spirits* you call your *ancestors*, are **demons**. Your deceased ancestors are not in this realm. They are not watching over you; they are not helping you in any way. Those are familiar *spirits*, and once you give way to them, they will take over your life in a most surprising and evil way. One way is that you'll end up talking to *familiar spirits* and demons rather than hearing or listening to the Holy Spirit. That is the same as going to psychics and diviners instead of listening to God. Second heaven intel and guidance is not God, is not of God, and it is not to be trusted.

Enter ye in at the strait gate: for wide *is* the gate, and broad *is* the way, that leadeth to destruction, and many there be which go in thereat: Because strait *is* the gate, and narrow *is* the way, which leadeth unto life, and few there be that find it. Beware of false prophets, which come to you in sheep's clothing, but inwardly they are ravening wolves. (Matthew 7:13-15)

Following is a brief discussion of some demonic *spirits* that work against marriage. Once you obey the Word of God, and resist these demonic *spirits* in Jesus Name, they will not be able to attack your marriage or block your getting married in the natural.

But regarding the dead you should pray:

98. Lord, any person who is now deceased who has married me in the spirit, for whatever reason they may have had, let that marriage be dissolved, in the Name of Jesus.

When people are involved in the occult, incest and anything evil and perverted is promoted by the kingdom of darkness. This is why people rape their own children. This is why people kill, even their own relatives; they are told to do this as sacrifice. W*hy*? So whatever thing they've gotten or are getting from the dark kingdom won't dry up for them-, greed, pride drives them. Even fear because if they've entered into a devil deal and do not bring a sacrifice, they will be the sacrifice. They are told to bring sacrifices, annually or with some type of regularity. Many times, the sacrifice called for is human.

99. By the power in the Blood of Jesus, Satan I am not your sacrifice, nor am I a candidate for sacrifice, in the Name of Jesus.

Also, by evil dedication, a person could be a candidate for sacrifice because they are owned by the devil, they have been dedicated or given to the devil by a parent, ancestor, or other evil blood relative or evil human agent.

Marry you, or kill you? Neither option is desirable if we are talking about the devil or any of his evil agents.

Jesus Christ is the only way out of evil dedication.

Spirit of Seduction

Now the Spirit speaketh expressly, that in the latter times some shall depart from the faith, giving heed to seducing spirits, and doctrines of devils; Speaking lies in hypocrisy; having their conscience seared with a hot iron; Forbidding to marry, and commanding to abstain from meats, which God hath created to be received with thanksgiving of them which believe and know the truth. (1 Timothy 4:1-3)

Works of the *spirit of seduction*:

- To keep a person unmarried.

- This *spirit* convinces a person that it is better to stay unmarried for any number of reasons.

- To find any excuse to divorce or to break up serious interpersonal relationships readily and often.

- To abandon spouse for selfish pleasures

- To diss (snub) God.

- Pits the genders against each other. Treats the opposite gender as evil, as the enemy, or as an opponent.

- Denies the importance of marriage.

- Rejection of traditional gender roles in marriage.

If one is a feminist, a pro male person is called a masculist. This takes things to a whole other level. The masculist is someone who advocates for men's rights, as if no one has rights anymore? What is this about? Competition? Extreme competition? Can't we just go with human rights? Or are males and females not both humans?

In a marriage the two should become one, so how will that happen with two factions within a marriage and a house? Factions and all of the above is works of the flesh.

Whoredoms

Whoredoms is really the strongman that houses the *spirit of seduction*. I wrote an entire book about this entitled, **Seducing Spirits: Idolatry & Whoredoms.** Practicing *whoredoms* means both idolatry toward God and also infidelity in relationships, especially the matrimonial relationship. It causes people to go a-*whoring* and break up their own relationships and marriages. All the while you think this running around is your idea, but it is not. That *spirit*, once in a person, will drive them into the streets until his spouse leaves him, or it pulls him away from his own family who he believes he loves. He may not know why he left them in the first place.

Idolatry and *whoredoms* travel together. If you see a person who is idolatrous, it is only a matter of time before the other *spirits* show themselves in this person's behavior. If a person cannot be true to God who has a Heaven to put them in and the keys and authority over Hell, what do you think will make them into a good spouse? I ask this question regarding humans in the natural, as well as demons in the spirit. You already know the answer to the demons in the spirit question. Now, consider the other and get ready to pray for your beloved if they are encumbered with these *spirits*.

The person under influence of this strongman/*spirits* will be driven to:

- Adultery
- Fornication
- Pornography,
- Sexting- sending indecent pictures.
- Idolatry against God.

If you suffer under these *spirits*, admit your problem, especially if you have seen it down your bloodline, and get deliverance.

(Some of this chapter taken from or inspired by: https://www.marvellousarunda.com/p/the-reality-of-spiritual-spouses)

Spirit of Divination

Divination doesn't just lead to *whoredoms* and adultery, it **is** *whoredoms* and adultery because the diviner and whomever has visited and paid that sorcerer is trying to get from another source what they should be getting from God.

This is straight up idolatry. Often, it looks like this:

- Seeking other *spirits* through horoscope, voodoo, obeah, spiritism, psychics, and lucky charms.
- Burning incense, special baths, magic gems, etc
- Witchcraft, Wicca
- Dating or marrying by superstition, horoscopes and zodiac signs.

(Some of this section was inspired by or used from :

https://www.revivalarrows.com/blog/4-demons-against-marriages)

Deliverance

Forgiveness is deliverance. Unforgiveness leads to captivity. Of course, the one not forgiving believes that the person they are not forgiving will go into captivity and "God" will get them. But, really the person who doesn't forgive goes into captivity, where the devil will get them.

If Jesus has the power of forgiveness on Earth and we are in Christ, then what we remit will be remitted, what we forgive will be forgiven. Therefore, saints of God, if we are the person who has nominated someone else for captivity by refusing to forgive them, we will be sad to see how regularly this will backfire on us.

However, when we forgive them, we no longer become a candidate for captivity. We can then walk out of spiritual lockdown.

Were *they* ever in captivity? It depends on God and that intended victim's relationship with God. If you think your unforgiveness is so strong and it is like wiry cords or fiery serpents that can lasso and tie up another human and then incarcerate them, then you have a vivid imagination.

The first major tenet of Christianity is forgiveness. Anyone who forgets this needs to have their walk with Christ checked.

An evil soul tie may be because of something negative, such as unforgiveness. You are thinking on the person all day – because you believe you hate them. But any evil soul tie, ties up a person—it binds them, at least that is the goal. However, if they did nothing to us – but they were called away, walked away, left for unknown and unseen reasons, we take them and ourselves out of any potential lockdown by forgiving them. Forgiveness is deliverance.

Grief—longstanding grief is unforgiveness. We are not forgiving the person for leaving. If we don't know how to forgive a person for dying, then we have a real problem.

Listen to this selfishness: I didn't forgive a person for breaking up with me because I didn't want him to break up with me. So, I had, in the spirit, created a soul tie with this person. Well, that's how it started, then it evolved into unforgiveness, or maybe it was always unforgiveness. No, I wasn't jealous of whomever he was with. I was angry with him and was unforgiving toward him--, although he never knew it. Here's the most selfish part: when my life wasn't working the way I thought it should be working, I blamed him because I had imagined how my life would have been *with* him, versus without him.

In my selfishness, I left God out of the whole equation, not realizing that God could have been showing me Mercy because with this guy, my life may have been worse, but did I know that? No, my imagination was running this. Also, I didn't know how this guy's life was going because we were no longer in touch, but I supposed he was fine, and I wasn't. This is pure ignorance on my part.

Finally, it dawned on me that maybe he wasn't okay either. Perhaps whatever caused us to break apart hurt both of us. Perhaps I was blessed to realize it and maybe he wasn't. Perhaps I was also blessed to know what to do, but he didn't. Perhaps it was my responsibility to do something about it, in prayer and warfare, but at that time, I didn't. I remained miserable and blaming him for things he had no part in, really.

But the reason for our break up may have been far more complicated than a twenty-something's brain can fathom. The problem could have been evil dedication on his side, or on my side as well. This is what they may call star-crossed lovers, those who want to be together, but something other worldly seems to be blocking them.

The person who is most spiritual must do what he or she knows to do, that is be constant in prayer. But he wasn't my spouse, so I had limited authority to actually pray for him.

Which brings us to this question: **Who can you really pray for?**

Regarding that unforgiveness and soul tie, once I came to myself and listened to the Spirit of God, there was deliverance because I forgave. I forgave him, whether he really did anything or not. I cast down my stupid imaginations. I stopped the blame game; I faced reality; I forgave myself and my own choices, and there was deliverance. Amen.

Prayer Authority

I was in serious warfare the other night and was interrupted briefly by the entity I was praying against--, most likely. The question put to me was, *Why was I praying for the person I was praying for?*

I answered in the same breath, *"I am related by blood to this person, therefore I have authority even responsibility to pray for them."*

Cain smart-mouthed God by asking if he (Cain) was his brother's keeper. The answer is yes, we have responsibility and authority to pray for those in our bloodline, unless they specifically tell us <u>not</u> to pray for them.

When you pray for someone who doesn't want to be prayed for that is witchcraft. If you are praying for something or in some way other than what and how they want you to pray for them, that is also witchcraft. If someone--, a relative or not, asks you to pray for them, then you have been granted authority to pray for them. It is on you, however, to ask them, How shall I pray for you? In other words, What do you want from God? The person may want healing. Find out what healing means to them. Is it medicine? Is it surgery? Is it divine healing with no medicine and no surgery? How do they want you to pray? Find out before praying, else if you are not in agreement with them, you may be hurting their prayer life rather than helping them.

Find out what the person wants you to pray on their behalf. Is what they are seeking God about godly? Or is it ungodly? If Sister Sally wants Sister Barbara's husband to leave Barbara and become Sally's husband – that is also witchcraft, you don't get into that.

If a person is your blood relative, especially your child, or your parent or sibling, you may pray for them. Your spouse is your blood relative. Your ex-spouse? If your covenant has been spiritually broken as well as legally broken then keep your mouth off of their life, unless it is for good, according to the Word of God, if you two share children. Else, let them be.

Notice that Jesus even asked those who came to Him for healing or deliverance, if they wanted to be made whole, or something to that effect. That is like saying, Are you here to be healed? Are you here for deliverance. Although we think it is implied because they got in the prayer line, some agreement still had to take place before even Jesus proceeded.

The Lord has given me a Word that **He will make me *single*.** The Lord sends His Word to His people. What do we do next? We agree with it. What God wants for me, I also want for myself, so I will agree with it. I will agree in prayers, decrees, and declarations. I will search the Bible to find that Word and study how it was effected in the Good Book. I will continue mentioning this to the Lord in prayer and ask the Holy Spirit to reveal anything else I need to know about this Word. In faith, I count this as done, to the Glory of God, even if it has not yet manifested.

Single to Be Married, or *Just* Single?

Everyone you were *promised to* could have already married you, spiritually speaking.

Tom thumb weddings were a thing back in the day. People and cultures have all kinds of traditions.

Making the word of God of none effect through your tradition, which ye have delivered: and many such like things do ye.
(Matthew 9:13)

A Tom Thumb wedding-, kids are so cute. Did the grown ups know what they were doing, or not? Cute as it may be, how many kids internalized this and believed they were married for real? How many never said another word about this event, but still believed silently that they were married? Words and events can be taken in a myriad of ways by different people. It's like watching a sitcom, what adults know to be humorous and may laugh at a child will believe it is true and a way of life. A child doesn't have the capacity and life experience to understand what is make-believe and what is not. Kids and the immature are very literal. How many little boys think they can fly? How many little girls grow up still waiting on Prince Charming? They may reject every normal suitor during the marrying years waiting on some fairy tale perfect person.

If a person is married emotionally or mentally, they will be throwing out hands off, and not available signals everywhere they go. This will turn off and reroute potential suitors.
.

You may have married anyone or everyone you **pretended** to marry- , say in the school or college play. If you're an actor, for example, you may have *married* a whole lot of people already. Did you consummate these marriages? You may not be an actor, but every time you consummated the marriage act, you got married again. Have you divorced any previous "spouses" first, before marrying the next one?

Everyone <u>you</u> claimed as a spouse: *I'm telling you that boy is fine, I'm going to marry him. That's my husband.* You may be spiritually married because of those words.

Everyone who claimed you as a spouse. *Look at that girl – that's my wife and I'm not going to stop until I marry her.* People you don't even know may be "spiritually" married to you.

Worse, someone you dated who has vowed and sworn never to let you go may still be spiritually married to you.

Why are all these above scenarios dangerous, when nobody got married in the natural world? Nobody married anyone, legally, so what's the problem?

Thy kingdom come, Thy will be done in earth, as it is in heaven. (Matthew 6:10)

What happens--, what **really** happens, happens in the spirit –, first, then it comes into the natural realm. Which one does God recognize? People think that when something happens in the natural, that is when it really happens, and that is where it **only** happens. So, which laws do we obey? Spiritual laws, or natural laws?

Both. We obey spiritual laws, but we do not neglect natural authority, natural governance, civil laws. You may argue that only good things happen in Heaven, so it's okay if that comes to Earth and into your life. God's Heaven, yes. But the devil is in second heaven, and don't you think a legalist, which the devil is, will try to appropriate that principle for his kingdom? Therefore, he is ever trying to make bad things happen in second heaven, and if you don't know anything about it, or don't do something about it, then it will to manifest in your life. This is why all these spiritual marriages are bad, very bad. This is why you must get out of every spiritual marriage.

I heard a grown man say just the other day that there is no such thing as germs, because he has never seen one. The spiritual world is smaller and less visible than a germ. At least with a good microscope you can see a germ, even in the natural. There is no *scope* to see into the spiritual realm except by the gift of God when one is given spiritual vision. Discernment also is a way to know what is going on spiritually.

Well, that grown man has never "seen" a spirit; he's never *seen* God. Maybe he has never heard of God; he doesn't seem to be one who serves God, else he wouldn't doubt the unseen world. So, he's living his carnal, flesh life using his natural eyes only.

Won't he be surprised in the end?

So, getting married spiritually is invisible, but you must know the signs. By saying you are married, or playacting in a wedding or saying over and over and over that you want to marry so and so because he's so cute is possibly how it happened to you. If it is something the devil set up and you did nothing about it, then it would stand. It stands until you do something about it.

Spiritually married is not that a human person actually married you, but it was an opportunity for a devil, demon or evil *spirit* to insert themselves into the "covenant" you were making with your juvenile, careless, or lust-filled words, and marry you. **Devil proof your words, always.**

Until you learn how to devil proof your words, maybe you could start with limiting how many words you actually speak. Everything that you say and do is not neutral, or no harm done – there is a binary choice, either God is in it, or God is not in it. God protects us from a million harms, and maybe even every day. The reckless words that we speak and hear and do nothing about are things that can harm, reroute, redirect, or even reprogram our lives or the lives of our children and their children.

We will have to give an account of every word we speak, and being able to make covenants--, good or bad, with our words, is one reason why.

The devil is default in the Earth, so if God is not in a thing, then the devil has authority to be in it or get in whatever deal, contract, or covenant you are making.

Puppy Love 2.0

There was that guy who sat by you on the school bus when you were ten and he was in high school and thought you were the cutest. But you have come to realize now that you're wiser, that he was just playing with you. But at that time, you thought he was serious. Every day he said, "You're so pretty. He said, "You're my girlfriend. He said, "I'm going to marry you."

You liked him because he was so nice to you, and you were ten. Somehow, he found out that you share the same birthday, so you saved him a seat every day. Really, he was nice to you, like a big brother and he paid you a lot of attention. When you're ten, isn't that what a boyfriend is? Someone who is not your relative who is friendly and pays attention to you? People of God, you do not know how anyone will internalize your words and actions toward them, good or bad, to the negative or the positive. So be very wise in interacting with people, especially young people.

Folks, it depends on who people are... yes words matter, but they especially matter out of the mouth of saved people. It especially matters out of the mouths of prophets. What was the spiritual designation of that guy who sat by you the entire school year and thought you were so cute when you were 10? Was he a prophet and didn't yet know it? Were you? Words have weight, my friends.

Neither filthiness, nor foolish talking, nor jesting, which are not convenient: but rather giving of thanks. (Ephesians 5:4)

By the time you were 11 he had graduated high school, gone on to college and later you heard that he had married someone you didn't even know. That was devastating news to you. You cried, but just a little bit because you secretly were waiting to grow up so you could marry him. In your childish mind, you thought he would wait for you.

What is **your** spiritual *designation*? Who are you to God? What weight do your words carry?

Thou art snared with the words of thy mouth, thou art taken with the words of thy mouth. (Proverbs 6:2)

This man has grown up and matured to be quite a man of God. The gifts of God are without repentance, so his words may have had a spiritual impact back then, especially because of the repetition of those spoken words. Still this fellow had a bunch of brothers and no sisters, so he may have "adopted" this cute 10-year-old girl as a little sister. But did she know that? And, those were not the words spoken out of his mouth.

Did they marry you, *spiritually*? Did you really marry them spiritually speaking? In the natural, you did not marry one another, but in the spirit a *wringer* could have been sent in and one or both of you may have gotten married in the spirit, but not to each other, that school year when you were ten. Especially if *spirit spouse* or something like that was in either or both bloodlines, those words spoken constituted what those demon *spirits* wanted or needed to hear to rope you and your next three generations into a spirit marriage, unless you wise up and break the evil covenant that allows for the spiritual marriage.

Spirit spouse is not just marrying you; it is marrying **your bloodline and everyone in it**--, male or female, male *and* female. *Spirit spouse* is no respecter of age, and it is no respecter of gender, either. It will marry a newborn; it will marry you in the womb. By evil dedication you could have been married at conception. By bloodline ancestral iniquity, you could have been dedicated and married 400 years before you were ever conceived or born. If there is an ancestral *spirit spouse* that entity has been in your family for ages.

Don't you think it's time to divorce it?

Folks, step up your prayer life especially as it concerns your children, there may be a real reason why they fight sleep and don't want to go to bed at night, but they don't have the vocabulary to tell you what's going on. *There's a monster in my room*, could mean nothing, or it could mean everything when your child tells you that. Don't dismiss it. Pray over your child, especially at bed and sleep times.

Divorce In the Courts of Heaven

99. Lord, I ask you today that I divorce the strongman, in the Name of Jesus.
100.   Let there be a divorce now, on the gates of my eyes, on the gates of my body, soul, and spirit.
101.   I divorce him now. I divorce the strongman, in the Name of Jesus.
102.   I am divorcing Satan, the strongman of my family, bloodline, in the Name of Jesus.
103.   Any network that I have ever gotten myself into, any alliances, evil covenants, groups that I ever got involved in, I get out now, by the power in the Blood of Jesus.
104.   I break every evil covenant, and I dismantle every curse that has come over my life and my family, in the Name of Jesus. .

105.   I divorce the strongman, in the Name of Jesus.

106.   I divorce him today, in the Name of Jesus.

107.   As the parent I take my authority to command a divorce from the strongman on behalf of my children, in Jesus' Name.

A *spirit spouse* is a rapist. Break every soul tie with the rapist. Disallow the rapist into your life because that rapist will open the door to other rapists and other *spirits* in the realms of darkness. DIVORCE the rapist – no matter who it is.

108.   I break every soul tie with every spiritual entity that has come into my life by any means, in the Name of Jesus.

109.   I break every soul tie with every dream attacker and spiritual rapist, in the Name of Jesus.

110.   I break every soul tie with any rapist in the natural world, in the Name of Jesus.

111.   Lord, I divorce every rapist, no matter the source, no matter the origin, no matter the duration of that evil entity in my life, in the Name of Jesus.

112.   Spiritual rapist, or astral projected rapist, I divorce you, in the Courts of Heaven today, in the Name of Jesus.

113.   I come boldly to the Throne of Grace, and I ask the Father to grant me divorce from all of these evil entities, in the Name of Jesus.

114.   I divorce Satan, by the power in the Blood of Jesus.

115.   I divorce the strongman; I divorce it now. (X7), in the Name of Jesus.

116.   I ask the Blood of Jesus to nullify and destroy any evil initiation that was conducted on me, on my life, in the Name of Jesus.

117.   I divorce it now, in the Name of Jesus.

118.   Blood of Jesus dismiss the initiation that was conducted on me, in the Name of Jesus.

119.   You *spirit*, you man, you woman, whoever you may be, today in the Name of Jesus, I divorce you. I divorce you, I divorce you, in the Name of Jesus.

120.   Lord, enter a decree of permanent divorce from these demons, in the Name of Jesus.

121.   I command a spiritual divorce, Lord, grant divorce from every evil spiritual entity, in the Name of Jesus.

122.   I divorce Satan, by the power in the Blood of Jesus.

123.   I divorce every evil human, astral projecting agent, in the Name of Jesus.
124.   I divorce the strongman, in the Name of Jesus.
125.   Blood of Jesus speak for me, dismiss, break every evil initiation, in the Name of Jesus.

(Some of the preceding prayers were adapted from James Kawalya)

126.   Wrong sex, I renounce you, I denounce you and every iniquity and evil contract you have allowed in my life, in the Name of Jesus.
127.   Illegal sex, I renounce you, I denounce you and every iniquity and evil contract you have allowed in my life, in the Name of Jesus
128.   Uncovenanted sex., I renounce you, I denounce you and every iniquity and evil contract you have allowed in my life, in the Name of Jesus.
129.   Unapproved sex, unsanctioned sex, nonconsensual sex, I renounce you, I denounce you and every iniquity and evil contract you have allowed in my life, in the Name of Jesus.
130.   In dreams, parties, in schools, at work, in hotels, at church… no matter where

wrong sex happened, I break your evil effects over my life, in the Name of Jesus.

131.   *Spirit spouse* and all of your effects get out of my mind, get out of my body, get out of the path of my destiny, in the Name of Jesus.

If you are married in the spirit that demon is territorial, jealous and wicked.

132.   I bind and paralyze the ability of that *spirit spouse* to do anything at all to me, in the Name of Jesus.

133.   I divorce the rapist, the abuser, the tormentor, in the Name of Jesus.

134.   I divorce the vector of evil *spirits* passed on to me to open the gates of hell against me, in the Name of Jesus.

135.   I divorce Satan and all your servants and all your serpents, in the Name of Jesus.

136.   I break all your covenants and contracts against me, in the Name of Jesus.

137.   I am married to Jesus. Jesus, as my legal husband, declare me single from every devil, demon, *familiar spirit,* strongman, principality, ruler, Satan, himself, every evil human agent, in the Name of Jesus. (X5). Amen.

What did the rapist say to you while you were in *the act*? Those were vows that he declared or wanted you to agree with. Those were oaths. You were initiated into something dark, and something evil. He tried to make you submit and impart a victim mentality to you. He tried to initiate you into occultism, witchcraft, or into becoming an altar yourself, one who transfers demons to others. You think it's promiscuity the reason you feel so lustful now? Call it what you want, you are on assignment to transfer demons from hell into others.

Ever notice how rapists and people such as that want the innocent? The young? They want the ones who have no demons, or certainly fewer demons than they do so they can dump demons on or into them. That is their demonic assignment.

What else did the rapist say, or have *you* to say during the act? Those words – are the names of other demons. This is sex magic and sexual conjuring. **Words that we think are profane words _are_ profane, and they are profane because they are the names of**

demons. Do not use those words, do not call those names.

They say rape is about power. Rape is spiritual; it is about darkness, and demons. Even those involved in money rituals are incentivized or required to rape or to have sex with as many as possible. Female or male. Males get raped more than you know, most often by other men. This is occultic. Who else would think of such a thing? Can a heterosexual man ever think that he needs to **divorce** another man who molested or raped him? But he must. No gender is off the hook. **If there was sex, there is a marriage.**

I speak to the *curious* who tried things as teens or in college, or even older people who knew you were not supposed to be doing *that*. In this way a female could be married to another female in the spirit, even if this was only a drunk or drugged up thing they did one night as a dare, or to please their perverted spouse or boyfriend. Divorce them.

The polygamy of this perversion is glaring. The perversion of this wicked spiritual polygamy is abhorrent. You must divorce all parties involved if you want to be spiritually free. Else, all *spirits* present at the event have full access to you from now on, as well as the other *spirits* they brought with them to the *party*.

And, **you** are the party.

Because of these freaky entanglements, you have been defiled and downgraded to be as a spiritual sexual dumpster. But I don't have to tell you that. Are you fighting off sex offenders in your dreams every night, or at least often?

Does it seem that you draw all kinds of *weird* into your natural life? Does *mess* seem to be attracted to you? Wrong people? Even people who seem great, but in no time it either falls apart or, even if you didn't find them to be the wrong person for your life, they suddenly disappeared, or you lost contact. Like, poof! Where did they go?

You can see what is happening to you in your dream life, and how you feel when you wake up in the morning. How you have lost control of your body, sexually. Marks on your body. Very irregular menses--, the demons want the blood, it renews covenant. Signs of sex in the morning when you wake up? Are you a good church girl who is being pimped out in the spirit at night and perhaps you have no idea that is happening? This certainly could put a reproach on you where you are not attractive to potential suitors.

Review the signs of such from earlier chapters. Another strong indication is that no one is interested in you romantically or as a marriage partner in the natural. You could be absolutely beautiful or daringly handsome, but no one is approaching you as a suitor or possible marriage partner. No one. A person could be spiritually defiled and have reproach on them that drives suitors away. If you've been *turned out* in the spirit, suitors will be turned off and away in the natural realm.

138.   *Spirit spouse* I am not your wife. I am not your husband. Stop calling me spouse; I am not your spouse, I'm not your relative, or friend. I hate you with perfect hate, in the Name of Jesus.

139.   If you're a demon, I cannot and can never be related to you, in Jesus' Name.

140.   If you are an agent of darkness, I have no communion with you; I am of the Light.

141.   Get back. Get up off of me! Get away from me, I divorce you, I divorce you, I divorce you, in the Name of Jesus.

142.   Evil human agents, ignorant human agents, friends, family, relatives – blood relatives, adopted relatives, ex's, in-laws, undercover haters, fake friends, colleagues, co-eds, co-workers— whomever you may be or whomever you may have been to me at the time, lose all power and control over me, in the Name of Jesus.

Sex In the Dream Prayers

If there is sex in the dream, then you are spiritually married. If there are attempts at sex in the dream you may have been spiritually married and gotten out of it, or an entity feels entitled and wants to ensnare you, or renew an old covenant. You can resist with words in the dream, you can resist with words and prayers in the natural, you can resist with praise and worship and fasting. Do all of that to fully resist. Remember to do all the disciplines of the Faith, including sacrifice and offerings.

143. Son of David, have Mercy on me, in the Name of Jesus.
144. I repent for every sin which has allowed sex in the dream to torment me in my sleep, in the Name of Jesus.
145. Lord, I repent for my parents and ancestors and ask you to remove all

iniquity from our bloodline, in the Jesus' Name.

146. Lord, forgive me of every sexual sin I have ever committed, in the Name of Jesus.

147. Forgive me for lust, pornography, masturbation of any kind, in Jesus' Name.

148. I renounce and denounce all sex magic, any conjuring of any demons, especially those called *spirit spouse*, in Jesus' Name.

149. Every personality that appears in my dream for sex, become impotent, in the Name of Jesus.

150. Every personality that appears in my dream for sex, the Lord Jesus rebuke you and the Sword of the Lord chase you away, in the Name of Jesus.

151. Lord, nail shut the coffin of *spirit spouse*, in the Name of Jesus.

152. Thank You, Lord, for total deliverance from *spirit spouse* in any form, in Jesus' Name.

153. I undo every spirit marriage I've agreed to knowingly and unknowingly.

154. Lord by forgiveness, I shut all open doors against the enemy.

155. Lord, forgive me for all works of the flesh that enslave me to Satan, in the Name of Jesus.

156. Blood of Jesus find and destroy all instruments of darkness assigned to oppress me in the dream, in Jesus' Name.

157. Evil visitors, night spouses, DIE, and rise no more, in the Name of Jesus.

158. Blood of Jesus incubate me with power against sex in the dream, in Jesus' Name.

159. Lord, any *spirit spouse* that has been sent to me by a witch, warlock, or evil agent of any kind, let them be returned to their sender, forever, in the Name of Jesus.

160. All virtues stolen from me by sex in the dream, I demand recovery of my blessings to seven-fold, in the Name of Jesus.

161. Every dark gift received in the dream from *spirit spouse*, as part of a marriage covenant, I return it now, in the Name of Jesus.

162. Dogs that appear in the sleep, in the dream, you represent *lust*, and covenant with a sex demon; I kill you with the Flaming Sword of the Lord.

163. Lord, empower me against powers of *spirit spouse*, in the Name of Jesus.

164. Lord, heal me of evil arrows sent via *spirit spouse*; return to sender, in Jesus' Name.

165. Lord, heal me from evil arrows, in the Name of Jesus.

166.   All anti-marriage, anti-breakthrough, and anti-progress because of sex in the dream, be canceled and reversed against me, in the Name of Jesus.

167.   Marks on, in or near me or my house by *spirit spouse* be erased by the power in the Blood of Jesus. I am not your candidate; I am not your victim, in the Name of Jesus.

168.   Blood of Jesus flush and purify me from all evil deposits, in the Name of Jesus.

169.   Blood of Jesus let every fluid stolen from me be burned up and utterly destroyed and useless to the thief, in the Name of Jesus.

Full prayer of Warfare Against Sex in the Dream on You Tube, prayed by this author:
https://www.youtube.com/watch?v=pOl9-JBdj_E&t=6345s

Warfare to Divorce & End Spirit Marriages

- Stop sinning
- Repent for your sins, and repent for ancestors that your bloodline iniquity will be purged.
- Divorce idol *gods*
- Break soul ties
- Break childhood vows.
- Break evil oaths
- Break evil covenants
- Pray against evil human agents
- Divorce *spirit spouse*

(The following prayer points in this chapter adapted from prayers by Pastor Ezekiel King https://a.co/d/6UdlIpl)

170. Lord Jesus, I repent for sexual immorality.
171. I repent for selling our children, boys, girls to demonic *spirits* by our own sins.

172.   Lord, we repent for having sex with dead bodies in the cemeteries.

173.   I repent for donating our sperm, eggs, and wombs to demonic altars.

174.   I am sorry for contacting evil altars for healing or deliverance.

175.   Lord, I am sorry for sleeping with harlots, for breaking my marriage,

176.   Lord, I repent for being an adulterer, a fornicator and a harlot, myself, in the Name of Jesus.

177.   Lord, I repent for divorce where any Godly covenant was broken. Lord, forgive me. I repent, in the Name of Jesus.

178.   I am sorry for attending demonic events.

179.   Lord, forgive me for opening the door to any demon in ignorance, disobedience, or rebellion, in the Name of Jesus.

180.   I repent for following prophets who we know are demonic.

181.   Jesus has the power to forgive on Earth-- Lord Jesus, forgive me today.

182.   Father I am sorry for masturbation, for using sex toys, sex magic, evil conjuring. I repent for sexual immorality, whether doing any of these things in ignorance, deceived by the world, or fully addicted;

Lord, forgive me, Lord. Forgive me, in the Name of Jesus.

183.   I am sorry for manipulating husbands, for manipulating wives to get our way, because that is witchcraft, in the Name of Jesus.

184.   Lord, forgive me for prostitution in or out of the marriage, in the Name of Jesus.

185.   Lord, forgive for seeking or entertaining the *gods* of our father's house, for seeking ancestral *spirits*. I repent, in the Name of Jesus.

186.   Lord, please forgive and remove the iniquity of all these sins, in the Name of Jesus.

Remember, we want to age gracefully. Toting around all that pain, emotional hurt, turmoil. What do you think your face will look like, eventually? What do you think people will see when they see you? No, they may not see the source of your pain, but they will see the pain.

A worse thing to do is to hold on to it.

The worst thing you can do is hold on to it and keep repeating it to people.

If possible, worse than that is holding on to it until you meet the man of your dreams for him to heal it. Even if he is a deliverance minister, *he* can't heal it; God, by His Spirit will be the healer, not a man. If he is a psychiatrist, he can't heal it. If he is a psychologist, he can't heal it. If he is a counselor, he cannot heal it. If he is a prophet, or intercessor, he won't heal it: at least the spiritual people are looking in the right direction for your spiritual, emotional, mental and sometimes bodily healing. HOWEVER: the average, normal, lay person – especially one who is not saved will not make it better, although he may spend a lifetime or two— yours and his trying to make it better for you.

Only God can save you, heal you, redeem you and cleanse you, and get you out of captivity. Don't lay that kind of bondage on a man, even if he wants to be a hero in your life. Don't save up all that hurt and pain and trauma waiting to find the person who will let you dump all that on him, every day, all day and sometimes all night.

Become single, yourself. Let the Lord make you single. Let the Lord make you single again if you have been encumbered with things and stuff and emotions, and baggage, and memories that you would rather be without.

187.   I break the power and control of every *spirit spouse* who believes it has married me, in the Name of Jesus.

188.   I reject and destroy every unholy marriage, in the Name of Jesus.

189.   I reject and remove every evil spiritual wedding ring on my finger, in the Name of Jesus.

190.   I break every evil soul tie, in the natural or in the spirit, in the Name of Jesus.

191.   Every demonic charge that leads or urges me to sin, break, by the power in the Blood of Jesus.

192.   I retrieve my destiny and glory, and blessings from every spiritual entity from my birth until now, in Jesus' Name.

193.   Every counterfeit promise, every demonic property given to me, to ratify evil covenants, I reject and return it, in the Name of Jesus.

194.   I destroy every evil covenant that led to spirit marriage, in the Name of Jesus.

195.   *Spirits of lust, greed, & seduction*, die out of me, in Jesus' Name.

196.   Any type of *spirit spouse*, I block you, in the Name of Jesus.

197.   Lord, by Fire, scatter every marine kingdom meeting concerning me, in the Name of Jesus.

198.   Every monitoring eye observing me, be blinded by Holy Ghost Fire, in the Name of Jesus.

199.   Every stolen blessing, property, and virtue, be returned to me seven-fold, in the Name of Jesus.

200.   Every *anti-marriage spirit*, every power opposing my natural marriage, fall down and die, in the Name of Jesus.

201.   Delayed marriage, jump out of my life, in the Name of Jesus.

202.   Any *spirit* that believes it has married me, I divorce you in the Courts of Heven. I divorce you, in the Name of Jesus.

203.   Every demonic shackle to hold me down, or stop me from living and fulfilling destiny, break, break, break, in the Name of Jesus.

204.   Every connection to any evil *spirit* or dark power and their networks, be broken off my life, in the Name of Jesus.

205.   Every anti-marriage power that is anti-finances, fall down and die, in the Name of Jesus.

206.   Every damage done to any aspect of my life, Lord, send Your healing balm and restore me, in the Name of Jesus.

207.   Lord, by Your restoring West Wind, send back into my life every good thing that has been taken from me, in the Name of Jesus.

208.   Every blocker *spirit* or power against me, lose your power, in the Name of Jesus.

209.   Strange man/strange woman, you will not destroy my marriage or marital destiny, in the Name of Jesus.

God Allows Divorce

God allowed divorce starting in the Old Testament because the men were killing their wives when they wanted a new wife. Yes, there is the crowd that says divorce is a sin. Breaking Godly covenant is not looked upon favorably by God, however there were instances in the Old Testament where a woman, yes, even a woman could divorce her husband.

- When he was not taking care of her financially, that is buying her clothes and food.
- And if he was not showing her *due benevolence.*
- As well, adultery by either party is grounds for divorce, even in the Bible.

If a man who has married a slave wife takes another wife for himself, he must not neglect the rights of the first wife to food, clothing, and sexual intimacy. If he fails in any of

these three obligations, she may leave as a free woman without making any payment.
Exodus 21:10-11)

Not only that, the Lord desires that we divorce idols, devils, and demons so we will be free to serve Him with our whole heart, and soul, and our being, so there are provisions for divorce. Of course we can divorce a devil, or demon—it's adultery in the first place—no one will ever tell you to keep fornicating, keep committing adultery, except the devil.

For a man to divorce a woman, or a woman to divorce a man, providing that spouse is fulfilling all their marital roles, just because of lusting for a different spouse is not what we are talking about here; that would be ungodly.

I particularly like Bride Movement's (Dan Duvall) prayers to divorce idols, so let's use that prayer and fill in the blanks with the known persons, former sexual partners, and ex's, and also entities to acquire divorces and achieve singleness. Also, on that same website pray the prayers against human persecutors (stalkers) so you can be free of those who have creepily *married* you that you don't know anything about. Be sure you repent of having done that to anyone yourself. You're not a stalker, are you? If you are, repent .https://bridemovement.com/freedom-from-human-persecutors-2-0/

Repent of worshipping at strange altars because when you do that, you also marry the priest or priestess of that altar. In addition, as if they are collecting email addresses to sell and make more money off of a customer, they then arrange for you to marry the demon or demons that sponsor them.

The Lord allows divorce; even though He hates broken Godly covenant, He allows divorce. So, let's pray to the Lord for divorce. We can list each known "marriage" singly or group them together. Don't be lazy, do as many as you know individually and at the end as you continue to repeat the prayer you may group all the unknown marriages together. When I first did the divorce the idols prayer, I did the whole list, one at a time. I must have prayed that prayer 30 or more times just in that one day. If you are serious you will pray against these spiritual marriages and divorce yourself of every evil entity, no matter how long it takes.

Become **single** and whole, freeing yourself from evil interlopers.

Grow Stronger, Live Longer

Grow stronger by reading your Bible out loud. Choose your Bible well. This is a powerful sequence of Psalms: Psalm 2, Psalm 24, Psalm 29, Psalm 35, Psalm 57, and Psalm 99.

Once delivered, unless the Lord has called you to be celibate, now that you are fully single with no attachments, no baggage and now ready to be married. If these matters are not corrected and settled before marriage, they will be the source of torment and turmoil within the marriage. Sadly, many can't see the spiritual source of their natural, marital problems, so they blame it on the other marriage partner, or on some behavior of that partner, or their in-laws or other friends and associates. *Baby, it's you* and your spiritual ***stuff***. Consider your own spiritual baggage before accusing anyone else.

Marry the one God chooses for you. be in a successful, happy marriage. Live longer and stronger. You will age gracefully and have a good life, a peaceful life.

Shun sin because in sin there are corrupt and surprise, hidden, spiritual marriages that will drain your virtues, your joy, your peace, even your strength, health and beauty.

Get Single

The Lord said that He will make me single, therefore He will, by His Spirit, amen. I rest in that, but I can do the work, the fasting, the prayer, the warfare, the study, Bible reading to agree with Him, and to facilitate and maintain my new *singleness*, to the Glory of God, amen.

For thy Maker *is* thine husband; the LORD of hosts *is* his name; and thy Redeemer the Holy One of Israel; The God of the whole earth shall he be called. (Isaiah 54:5)

210. Lord, grant me spiritual divorce from any and all spiritual entities or evil humans who have married me in the spirit, in Jesus' Name.

211. Grant divorce from ignorant humans who with their own words, and/or mine, have married me in the spirit, against my

knowledge or will, and thereby blocked my marital destiny, in Jesus' Name. Amen.

I asked more than one adult male if they will let their 25+ years old daughter ever get married, some say as they look at me surprised that they will. At least one father says, *No*.

Another father says of his 30-year-old daughter, *I'm not ready for that*. Could it be that these fathers have married their own daughters in the spirit and are blocking their daughter's chances of getting married in the natural? Another father has blocked his two daughters from marriage by more willful and occultic means. He may or may not have married them himself. However, he may have married them off to something or someone that they have absolutely no awareness of. Those girls all need to be made single so they can marry in the natural.

The thought that you may have to divorce a parent, or both parents, spiritually may seem strange, but really think about it. How many 'momma's boys' have you met? Daddy's girls? They talk about apron strings, it's more than that there is a strange spiritual connection that you may need to be free of to become single to become available for marriage in the natural realm. Sometimes these spiritual parent-to-child marriages are created by soulish or diabolical prayers such as a parent wishing a child would never grow up. Or a child wanting to stay a child always is a Peter Pan problem. Sometimes it is the parent who doesn't trust the child to ever leave home, or selfishly wants the child to stay home to take care of them in their old age. Then there is the parent who doesn't think that anyone---, anyone at all is good enough for their child. These are the makings of spiritual marriages, and these cords need to be broken so the adult child can go on and live their life.

Sometimes siblings have married one another, or one sibling has married the needier sib or sibs. These spiritual marriages block natural marriages. This is the spiritual fallout of the so-called, *close-knit family*. They may not even realize it, but they have created unusual alliances, and soul ties, perhaps around loss or pain. Few or none of them are married; if they are, they are not happily married, and the group may experience multiple divorces.

The Lord has told me that He is making me single. The Word of the Lord is here for you, as well, if you agree and desire to be single so that you may reach your true marital potential and destiny to the Glory of God. .

212.   I seal the declarations, decrees, prayers and words of this book across every era, age, realm, dimension, and timeline, past, present and future, to infinity, with the Blood of Jesus, and the Holy Spirit of Promise.

213.   Any retaliation against the author, the reader, the speaker, or anyone praying the prayers of this book, backfire against the retaliator, to infinity, and without Mercy, in the Name of Jesus.

AMEN.

Divorce Fallen Angels Prayer

"Father in Heaven, I come before you in the mighty Name of Jesus Christ and I renounce ___ and my ___ bloodline, genetics, ungodly DNA strands, bone marrow, cellular programming, anchors, and markers, and all the powers of darkness associated with this, and serve them a bill of divorce. I pull up the hidden documents detailing every covenant, contract, certificate, oath, and vow entangling me and command they be stamped with the Blood of Jesus...."

This prayer to divorce fallen angels and non-human entities starts on page 75 of his book, **Prayers that Shake Heaven and Earth**. To get and pray the rest of that prayer get Daniel Duvall's book. His book has prayers that are of a different level than the prayers in this book, but you may need to take it to that level, depending on your situation.

The prayers in this book, **Already Married in the Spirit:** *Why You May Not be Married in the Natural* are also very effective and should be prayed for your freedom, deliverance, and singleness. **Amen.**

Dear Reader:

Thank you for acquiring and reading this book. I pray it has set you free as it pertains to being burdened with a bunch of spouses that you may not have realized that you have.

Pray the prayers and let the Lord bring you to wholeness and singleness so you can worship and serve Him properly, as well so you can enter into marriage, be successful and happy in marriage and receive all the blessings that the Lord has for you, your marriage, and your family.

Shalom,

Dr. Marlene Miles

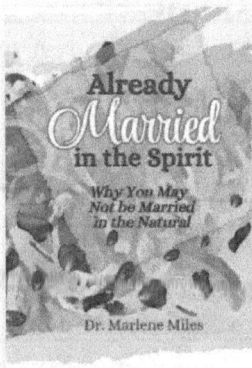

Prayerbooks by this author

While most books by this author have prayer points either throughout the book or at the end, there are some books that are only prayers. You just open up the book and pray. They are listed below:

Prayers Against Barrenness: *For Success in Business and Life*

Fruit of the Womb: *Prayers Against Barrenness*

Beauty Curses, *Warfare Prayers Against*
https://a.co/d/5Xlc20M

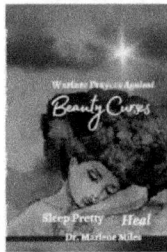

Courts of Marriage: Prayers for Marriage in the Courts of Heaven *(prayerbook)*
https://a.co/d/cNAdgAq

Courtroom Warfare @ Midnight
(prayerbook) https://a.co/d/5fc7Qdp

Demonic Cobwebs *(prayerbook)*
https://a.co/d/fp9Oa2H

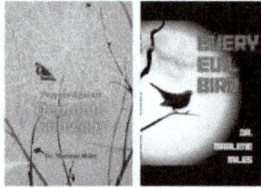

Every Evil Bird https://a.co/d/hF1kh1O

Gates of Thanksgiving

Spirits of Death, Hell & the Grave, Pass Over Me and My House

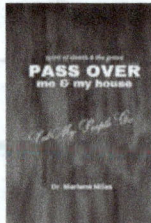

Throne of Grace: Courtroom Prayer

Warfare Prayer Against Poverty
https://a.co/d/bZ611Yu

Other books by this author

AK: The Adventures of the Agape Kid

Already Married in the Spirit: *Why You May Not Be Married in the Natural*

AMONG SOME THIEVES

Ancestral Powers

Anti-Marriage, *The Spirit of*

Backstabbers https://a.co/d/gi8iBxf

Barrenness, *Prayers Against* https://a.co/d/feUltIs

Battlefield of Marriage, *The*

Blindsided: *Has the Old Man Bewitched You?* https://a.co/d/5O2fLLR

Break Free from Collective Captivity

Casting Down Imaginations

Churchzilla, The Wanna-Be, Supposed-to-be Bride of Christ

Curses of Blind Men

Demonic Cobwebs (prayerbook)

Demonic Time Bombs

Demons Hate Questions

Devil Loves Trauma, *The*

Devil Weapons: Unforgiveness, Bitterness,…

The Devourers: Thieves of Darkness 2

Do Not Swear by the Moon

Don't Refuse Me, Lord (4 book series)

https://a.co/d/idP34LG

Dream Defilement

The Emptiers: *Thieves of Darkness, 1*
https://a.co/d/5I4n5mc

Evil Touch

Failed Assignment

Fantasy Spirit Spouse
https://a.co/d/hW7oYbX

FAT Demons (The): *Breaking Demonic Curses*

The Fold (5-book series)

- The Fold (Book 1)
- Name Your Seed (Book 2)

- The Poor Attitudes of Money (3)
- Do Not Orphan Your Seed (4)
- For the Sake of the Gospel (5)
- My Sowing Journal

Gang Ups: Touch Not God's Anointed

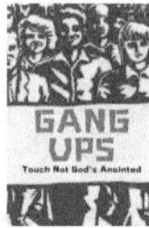

got HEALING? Verses for Life

got LOVE? Verses for Life

got HOPE? Verses for Life

got money? https://a.co/d/g2av41N

How to Dental Assist

How to Dental Assist2: Be Productive, Not Wasteful

I Take It Back

Legacy

Let Me Have A Dollar's Worth
https://a.co/d/h8F8XgE

Level the Playing Field

Living for the NOW of God

Lose My Location
https://a.co/d/crD6mV9

Man Safari, *The*

Marriage Ed. Rules of Engagement & Marriage

Made Perfect in Love

Money Hunters: Beware of Those

Money on the Altar https://a.co/d/4EqJ2Nr

Mulberry Tree https://a.co/d/9nR9rRb

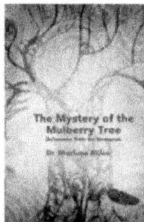

Motherboard (The) ~ *Soul Prosperity Series*

Name Your Seed

Occupy: *Until I Return*

Plantation Souls

Players Gonna Play

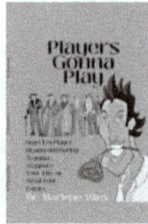

Power Money: Nine Times the Tithe

https://a.co/d/gRt41gy

The Power of Wealth *(forthcoming)*

Powers Above

The Robe, Part 1, The Lessons of Joseph

The Robe, Part II, The Lessons of Joseph

Seasons of Grief

Seasons of Waiting

Seasons of War

Second Marriage, Third--, *Any Marriage*

https://a.co/d/6m6GN4N

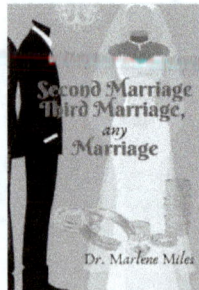

Sift You Like Wheat

Six Men Short: What Has Happened to all
the Men?

Soul Prosperity soul prosperity series 3

https://a.co/d/5p8YvCN

Souls Captivity soul prosperity series 2

The Spirit of Anti-Marriage

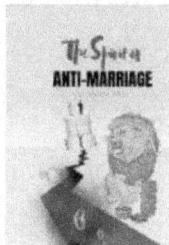

The Spirit of Poverty

StarStruck

SUNBLOCK

The Swallowers: *Thieves of Darkness*, 3

Take It Back

This Is NOT That: How to Keep Demons from Coming at You

Time Is of the Essence

Too Many Wives: *Why You Have Lady Problems*

Tormenting Spirits
https://a.co/d/dAogEJf

Toxic Souls

Triangular Power *(series)*

- Powers Above
- SUNBLOCK
- Do Not Swear by the Moon
- STARSTRUCK

Uncontested Doom

Unguarded Hours, *The*

Unseen Life, *The* (forthcoming)

Upgrade: How to Get Out of Survival Mode

- Toxic Souls (Book 2 of series)
- Legacy (Book 3 of series)

The Wasters: *Thieves of Darkness,* Bk 2
https://a.co/d/bUvI9Jo

What Have You to Declare? What Do You Have With You from Where You've Been?

When I Was A Child, *I Prayed As a Child*

When the Devourer is Rebuked

https://a.co/d/1HVv8oq

The Wilderness Romance *(series)* This series is about conducting a Godly relationship and marriage with someone who is a Wilderness person. It is about how to recognize it and navigate through it. These books are about how not to get caught up in such.

- *The Social Wilderness*
- *The Sexual Wilderness*
- *The Spiritual Wilderness*

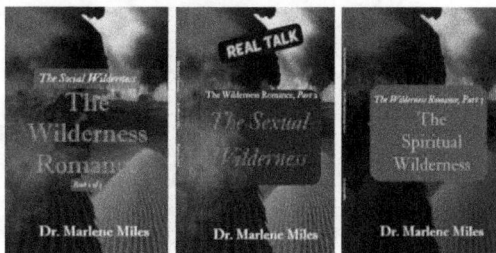

Other Series

The Fold (a series on Godly finances)
https://a.co/d/4hz3unj

Soul Prosperity Series https://a.co/d/bz2M42q

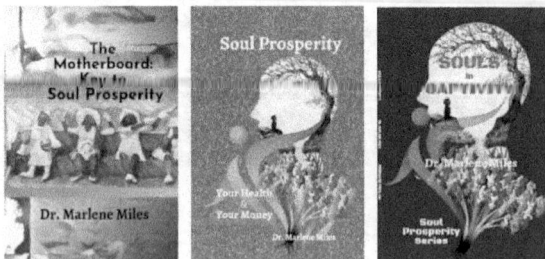

Spirit Spouse books

https://a.co/d/9VehDSo

https://a.co/d/97sKOwm

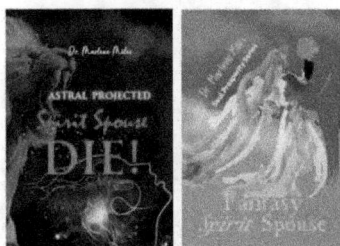

Thieves of Darkness series

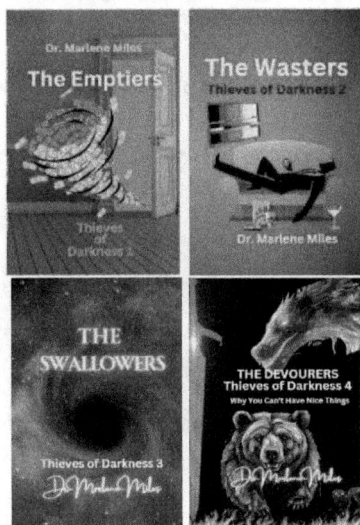

Triangular Powers https://a.co/d/aUCjAWC

Upgrade (series) *How to Get Out of Survival Mode*
https://a.co/d/aTERhX0

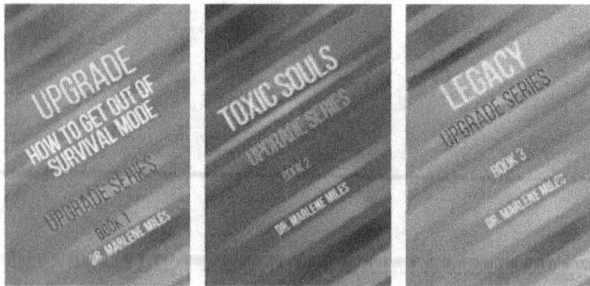

www.ingramcontent.com/pod-product-compliance
Lightning Source LLC
LaVergne TN
LVHW052029080426
835513LV00018B/2249